SPHINX

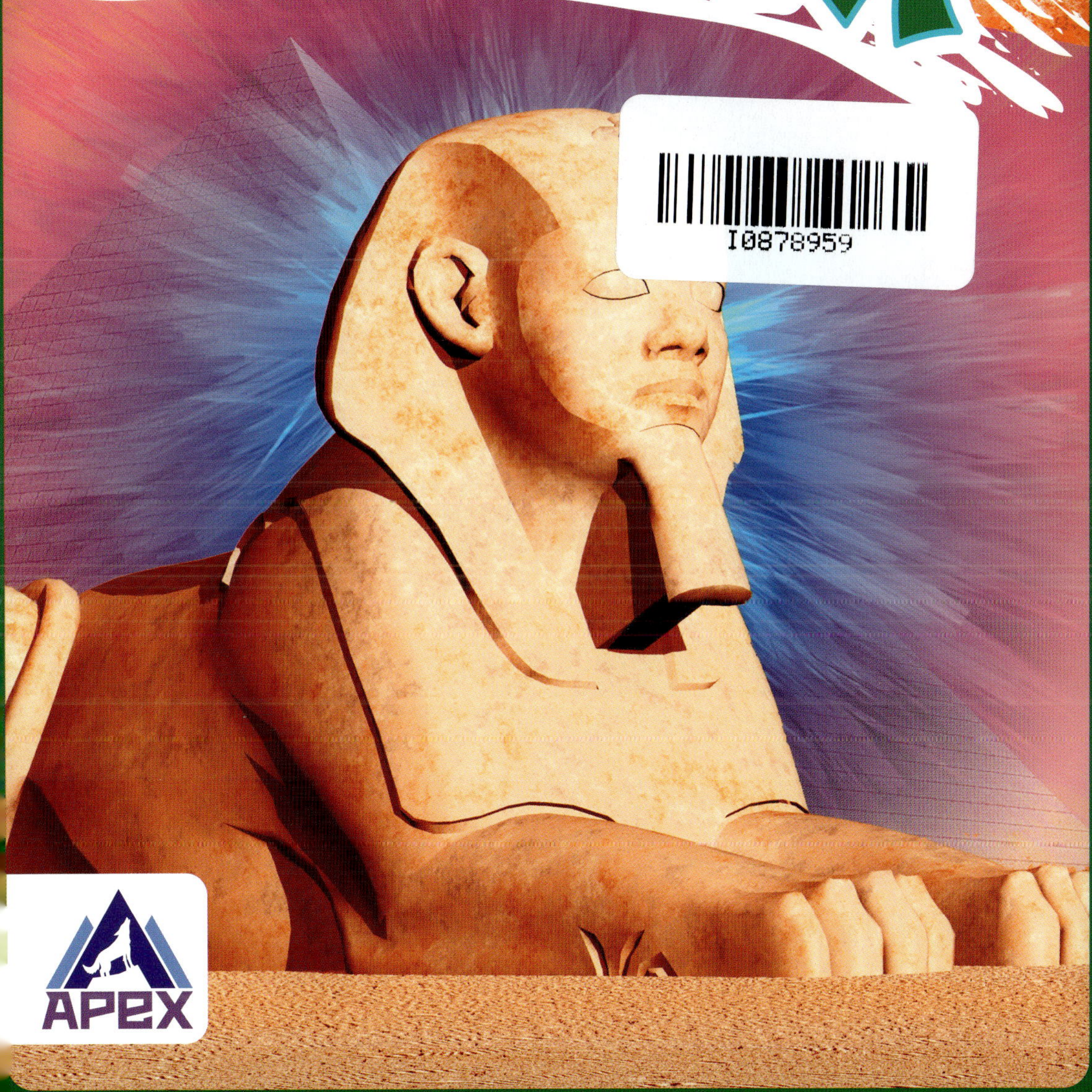

APEX

By Christine Ha

WWW.APEXEDITIONS.COM

Apex is distributed by North Star Editions:
sales@northstareditions.com | 888-417-0195

Produced for Apex by Red Line Editorial.

Photographs ©: Shutterstock Images, cover, 1, 4–5, 6, 7, 8–9, 10–11, 12–13, 14–15, 16–17, 18–19, 20, 22–23, 24, 25, 26–27, 29; iStockphoto, 21

Library of Congress Control Number: 2020952949

ISBN
978-1-63738-025-3 (hardcover)
978-1-63738-061-1 (paperback)
978-1-63738-130-4 (ebook pdf)
978-1-63738-097-0 (hosted ebook)

Printed in the United States of America
Mankato, MN
082021

NOTE TO PARENTS AND EDUCATORS

Apex books are designed to build literacy skills in striving readers. Exciting, high-interest content attracts and holds readers' attention. The text is carefully leveled to allow students to achieve success quickly. Additional features, such as bolded glossary words for difficult terms, help build comprehension.

TABLE OF CONTENTS

CHAPTER 1

GUARDING THE GATE

A sphinx sits by an **ancient** city's gate. A man tries to go past. The sphinx says he must answer a riddle first.

Gates helped control who could enter and exit ancient cities.

The riddle is tough. No one has solved it before. The man thinks long and hard. Finally, he gives his answer.

Carvings of sphinxes often decorated temples and tombs.

Some griffins have claws on their front feet.

In art, sphinxes often appear with griffins. A griffin is half lion and half eagle.

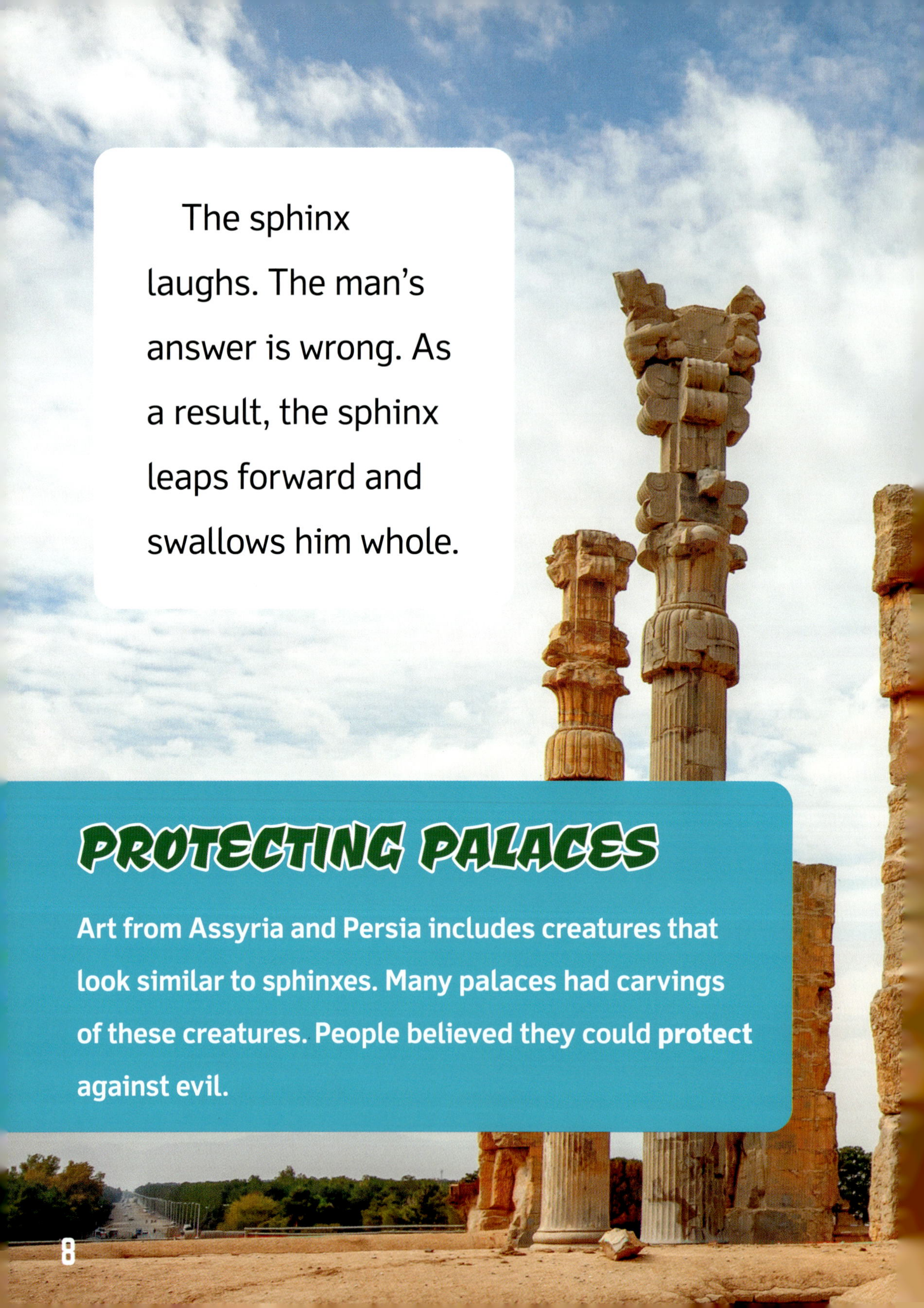

The sphinx laughs. The man's answer is wrong. As a result, the sphinx leaps forward and swallows him whole.

PROTECTING PALACES

Art from Assyria and Persia includes creatures that look similar to sphinxes. Many palaces had carvings of these creatures. People believed they could **protect** against evil.

Statues guard the gates to an ancient city in Iran.

CHAPTER 2

AN ANCIENT LEGEND

The sphinx is a **mythical** creature. It has a lion's body. It usually has a human head. But it can have the head of an animal.

Sphinxes often wear headdresses and crowns like the ones worn by Egypt's rulers.

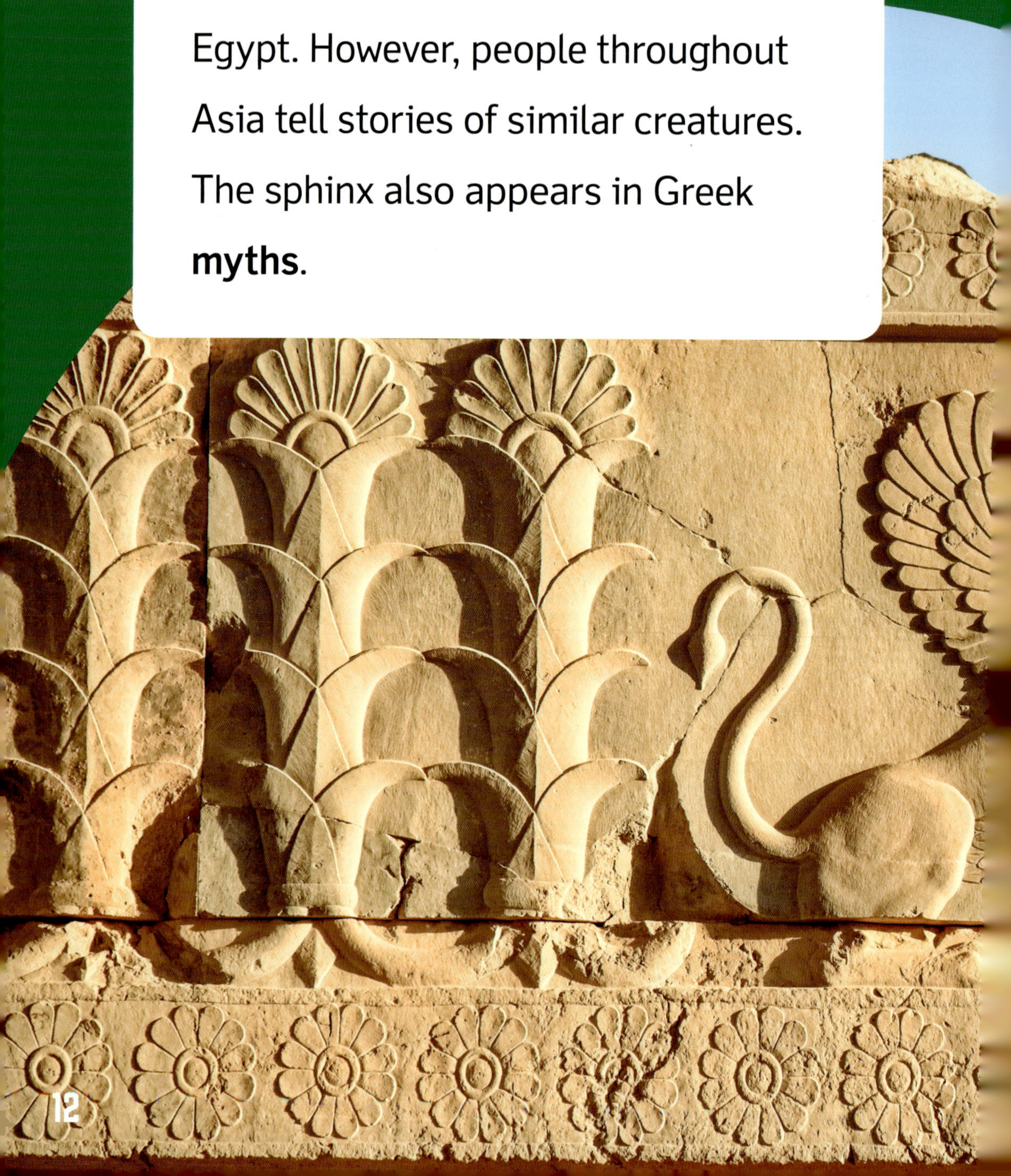

The sphinx comes from ancient Egypt. However, people throughout Asia tell stories of similar creatures. The sphinx also appears in Greek **myths**.

In some stories, the sphinx has a mane like a lion.

The lamassu is similar to the sphinx. It has a human head and the body of a lion or bull.

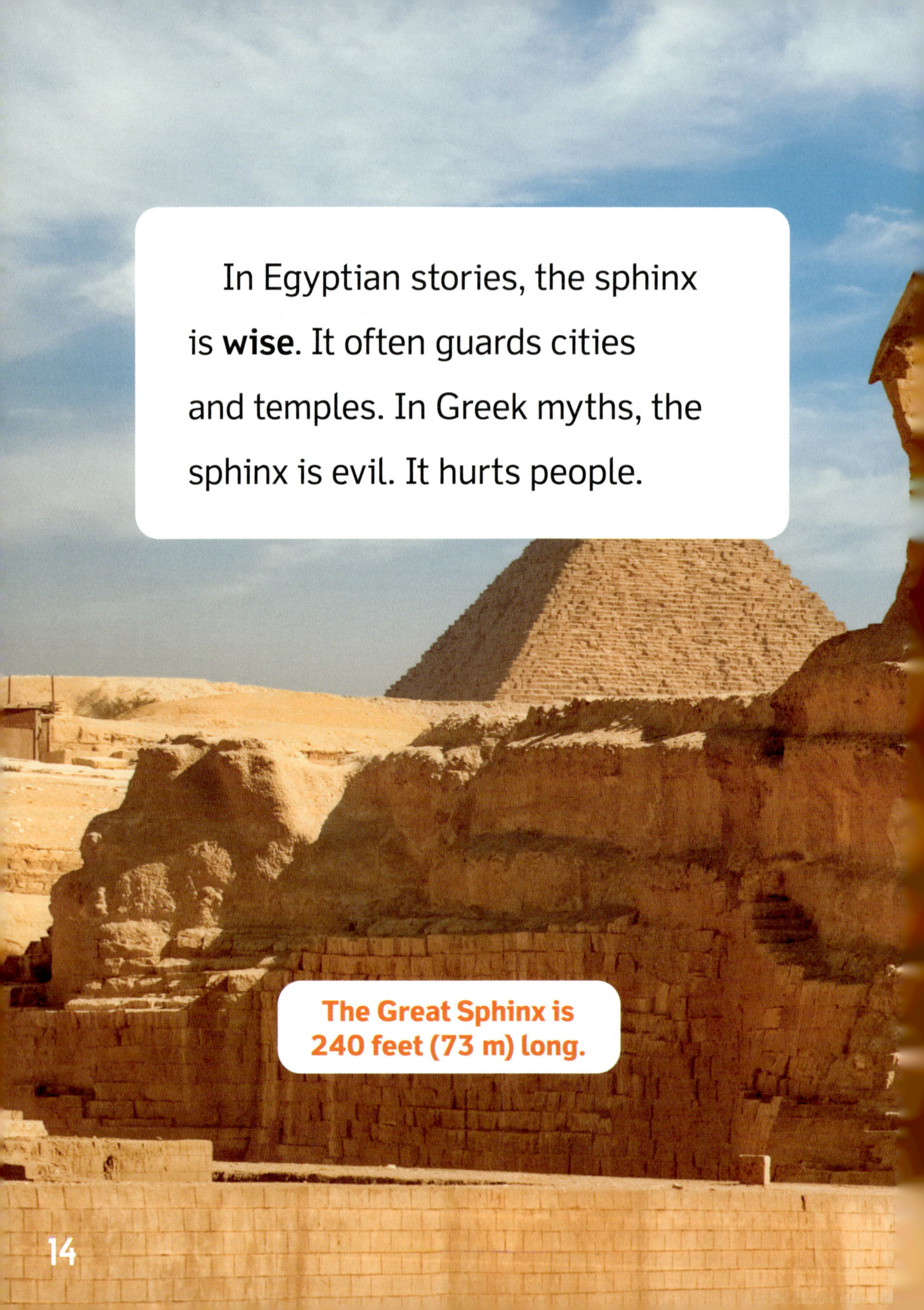

In Egyptian stories, the sphinx is **wise**. It often guards cities and temples. In Greek myths, the sphinx is evil. It hurts people.

The Great Sphinx is 240 feet (73 m) long.

THE GREAT SPHINX

The Great Sphinx is a huge statue in Egypt. It stands 66 feet (20 m) high. It was made thousands of years ago. But people can still visit it today.

CHAPTER 3

TRICKY RIDDLES

One sphinx **tormented** the city of Thebes. It made people answer a riddle. It asked what had four feet in the morning, two feet at noon, and three feet at night.

Several Greek myths take place in the city of Thebes.

Many people tried and
failed to guess the answer.
Finally, a hero solved it.

The hero Oedipus solved the sphinx's riddle.

The sphinx ate everyone who guessed wrong.

His answer was “a man.” A baby crawls on all fours. An adult walks on two legs. An old man uses a cane. Thanks to the hero, the city was saved.

The sphinx of Thebes caused a drought. The dry ground couldn’t grow enough food.

The sphinx left Thebes after a hero guessed the riddle's answer.

ANOTHER RIDDLE

Some stories add a second riddle. It asks about two sisters. The first gives birth to the second. The second does the same for the first. The answer is "day and night."

CHAPTER 4

THE LEGEND SPREADS

Ancient Egypt was very powerful. As a result, ideas from Egypt spread to other places. The sphinx is one example.

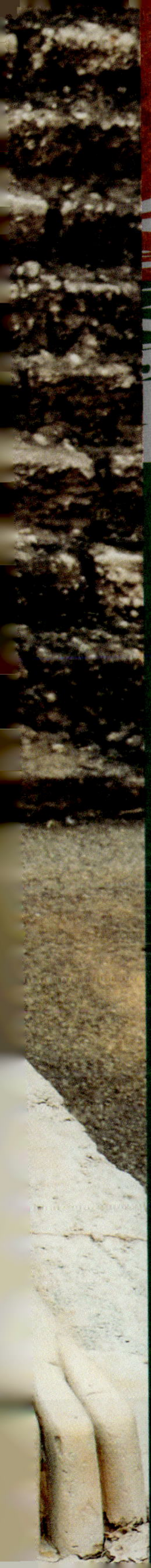

Sphinxes were often carved to have the faces of Egypt's rulers.

The creature's **traits** changed as the stories spread. Most sphinxes in Egypt were male. Sphinxes in Asia are female. And they often have wings.

Some sphinxes have the heads of rams.

In Egypt, the sphinx was a symbol of the king.

Thutmose was king of Egypt for about nine years.

A KING'S DREAM

A prince named Thutmose dreamed of a buried sphinx. The dream told him to dig it out of the sand. It said he'd rule Egypt if he did. This **prediction** came true.

In Greek myths, the sphinx has a woman's head. It has wings, too. But in these stories, the sphinx is **dangerous**.

Some Greek myths say the sphinx has a snake's tail.

People around the world copied the art and ideas of ancient Greece.

COMPREHENSION QUESTIONS

Write your answers on a separate piece of paper.

1. Write a few sentences describing the main ideas of Chapter 4.

2. Would you like to try answering a sphinx's riddle? Why or why not?

3. Where did legends of the sphinx begin?

  A. Egypt
  B. Persia
  C. Greece

4. Why would the ideas of a powerful country be likely to spread?

  A. The country would take over or trade with many areas around it.
  B. The country would keep all other people out.
  C. The country would try not to share its ideas.

5. What does **tough** mean in this book?

*The riddle is **tough**. No one has solved it before.*

A. hard to bend
B. easy to solve
C. hard to do or understand

6. What does **buried** mean in this book?

*A prince named Thutmose dreamed of a **buried** sphinx. The dream told him to dig it out of the sand.*

A. out in the open
B. high in the air
C. covered in dirt or sand

Answer key on page 32.

GLOSSARY

ancient

Very old or from long ago.

dangerous

Likely to cause problems or harm.

mythical

From stories or myths, not real life.

myths

Well-known stories from the past that often include magic.

prediction

A statement about what will happen in the future.

protect

To watch over or keep safe.

tormented

Hurt badly or caused great pain.

traits

Details that set a creature apart from others, such as how it looks or what it can do.

wise

Able to make good choices, often by knowing many things.

TO LEARN MORE

BOOKS

Gagne, Tammy. *Egyptian Gods, Heroes, and Mythology.* Minneapolis: Abdo Publishing, 2019.

Green, Sara. *Ancient Greece.* Minneapolis: Bellwether Media, 2020.

Nardo, Don. *Ancient Egypt.* Lake Elmo, MN: Focus Readers, 2020.

ONLINE RESOURCES

Visit **www.apexeditions.com** to find links and resources related to this title.

ABOUT THE AUTHOR

Christine Ha lives in Minnesota. She loves traveling and learning about the world. She hopes to visit Egypt one day to see the Great Sphinx.

INDEX

Answer Key:
1. Answers will vary, **2.** Answers will vary; **3.** A; **4.** A; **5.** C; **6.** C